D0479831

Contents

How Clean Can You Get?

How many times have you been told to use soap when washing? People have known for a very long time that water alone does not clean very well. You need soap. One legend claims that soap was first discovered about

3,000 years ago. At that time, Roman women washed their clothes in the Tiber River. They noticed that their clothes got especially clean when they were washed at the bottom of a hill called Sapo. The substance in the water that cleaned the clothes became known as soap, which was named after the hill.

The first use of soap actually goes back even further.

Directions for making soap have been found on clay tablets that are about 4,500 years old. These recipes called for mixing the ashes from wood fires with water. While the water was being boiled, fat from animals was added slowly. This recipe can still be used to make soap. However, this soap would be too harsh to use on the skin. It is good only for cleaning clothes.

You can buy soap for washing hands or for washing a car.

Since ancient times, many new recipes for making soap have been developed. Today, you can find many kinds of soap. Soaps are made for cleaning hands, faces, cars, pets, and clothes.

What is it about soap that makes it clean almost any-thing when it is added to water? To find the answer to this question, all you have to do is carry out the experiments in this book.

What Does Soap Do?

If you could look closely enough, you would see that water is made up of tiny particles. These particles are called **molecules**. Water molecules stick together. In fact, they stick together so well that it is hard to break them apart. One way to break them apart

Puddles form after it rains because water molecules stick together.

is by adding soap. See what happens when soap starts breaking apart water molecules.

Breaking the Tension

You will need:
- scissors
- index card
- sink
- liquid soap

Cut the card into the shape of a boat as shown in the picture. Fill the sink with water. Gently lower your boat onto the water so that it floats. Does your boat move through the water? Add several drops of liquid soap into the cut-out area in the back of your boat. Watch what happens.

Surface tension forms a thin skin that allows this water strider to walk on water.

When you first place your boat in the sink, the water molecules are sticking together. The molecules stick together so well that they made a very thin skin on the surface. You can think of this skin as a piece of tissue paper that lays on the surface of the water. This skin is the result of what scientists call **surface tension**.

When you add the soap, the water molecules start moving away from each other quickly. As the water molecules start moving, they push the boat. Soap breaks the surface tension of water so that the molecules can move apart. But how does soap clean your hands or your clothes?

Experiment 2

Washing Away the Dirt

Fill one of the jars with water. Add several drops of food coloring. Put on the lid and shake the jar to mix the food coloring and the water. Then pour half of this colored water into the other jar.

Tilt one of the jars. Slowly pour a small amount of the cooking oil down the side of the jar. The oil should float on the water. Continue adding the oil until the

14

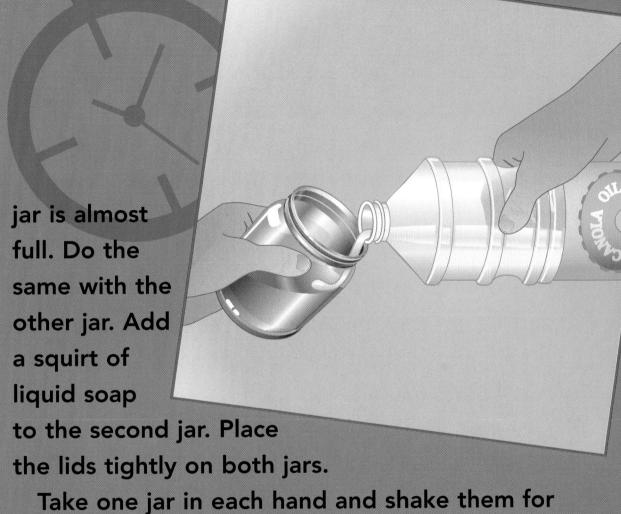

jar is almost full. Do the same with the other jar. Add a squirt of liquid soap to the second jar. Place the lids tightly on both jars.

Take one jar in each hand and shake them for thirty seconds. Then place both jars on a table or counter top. Watch what happens in each jar.

Shaking the jars mixes the oil and water. However, oil and water normally do not stay mixed. So as soon as you stop shaking the jar, the oil and water begin to separate in the jar without the soap. They form two separate layers, just as they did when you first poured in the oil. But why do the oil and water stay mixed in the jar with soap?

Like water, soap is made of molecules. A soap molecule is long. One end grabs on to water. The other end grabs on to oil. By holding on to both water and oil, soap can keep the two mixed.

A soap molecule works the same way when it cleans. One end grabs on to the dirt,

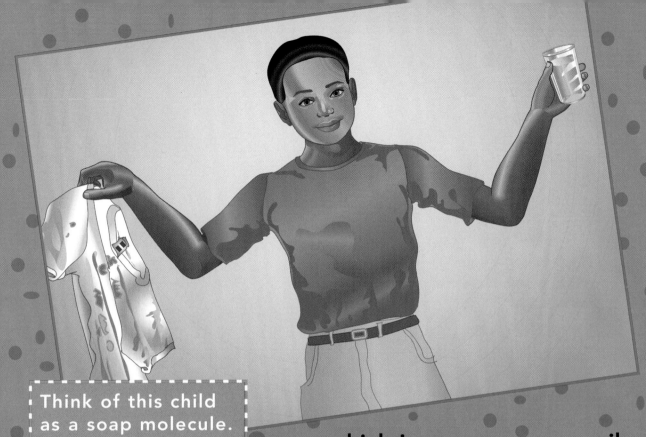

Think of this child as a soap molecule. By grabbing on to water on one side and dirt on the other, soap can mix the two.

which is a grease or an oil. The other end grabs on to water. As more water is added, it washes away the dirt. Without the soap, the water could not mix with the dirt to wash it away. But soap may not always get things clean. See how soap acts in different kinds of water.

Experiment 3

Making Suds

You will need:
- masking tape
- two small jars with lids
- marker
- distilled water
  (available at a pharmacy)
- teaspoon
- Epsom salts
  (available at a pharmacy)
- liquid soap
- clock or watch with
  second hand
- ruler

Tear off two pieces of tape. Write **"distilled water"** on one piece of tape and **"hard water"** on the other piece. Place a piece of tape on each jar. Fill the first jar halfway with distilled water. Fill the other jar halfway with tap water. Add a teaspoon of Epsom salts to the jar labeled "hard water" and stir for two minutes.

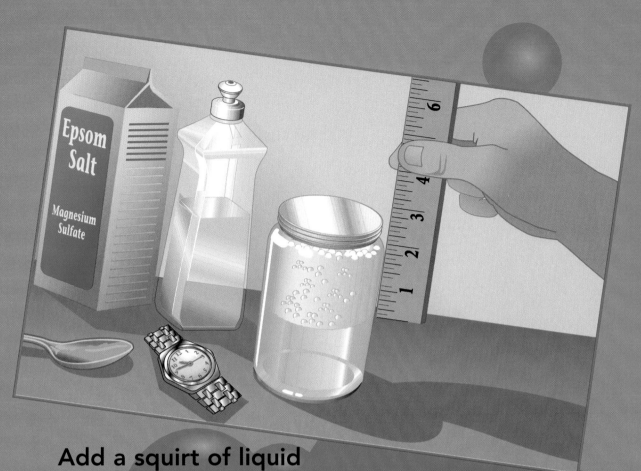

Add a squirt of liquid
soap to each jar. Place the lids on the jars
tightly. Shake the jar with the distilled water for
one minute. Then place the jar on a table or
counter top. Measure the height of the suds
layer in the jar. Do the same with the other jar.
Which jar produces more suds?

Which jar contains
the distilled water?

The jar with the distilled water produces more suds. Distilled water is pure water. The purer the water, the more suds soap can make in it. The more suds it makes, the better soap cleans. The jar with the Epsom salts produces fewer suds. The water in this jar contains a lot of salts. Water with salts in it is called hard water. Soap cannot make as many suds in hard water, so it cannot clean as well in hard water. Is cleaning the only thing you can do with soap?

What Else Can Soap Do?

You probably have gotten soap in your eyes when washing your face. If you have, then you know that soap can sting your eyes. Soap stings because of a chemical substance it contains. This substance irritates the tiny nerves near your eyes.

Whenever these nerves are
irritated, you feel a sting.
What kind of chemical in soap
can sting your eyes?

Changing Colors

You will need:
- adult helper
- sharp knife
- cutting board
- red cabbage
- pot
- stove
- measuring cup
- three small glasses
- white vinegar
- tablespoon
- baking soda
- liquid soap

Ask an adult to help you prepare a liquid from red cabbage. Chop up about a quarter of the red cabbage. Place the chopped leaves into a pot and then cover with water. Gently boil the leaves until the water turns a dark purplish color. Let the water cool. Carefully pour the cabbage juice into a measuring cup.

Chop the cabbage into small pieces

Pour equal amounts of cabbage juice into three glasses. Add 1/4 cup (2 ounces or 60 milliliters) of vinegar to one glass. What color does the cabbage juice turn? Add 2 tablespoons of baking soda to another glass and stir. What color does the cabbage juice turn this time? Finally, add 1/4 cup (2 oz or 60 ml) of liquid soap to the last glass and stir. Compare the color you get when adding soap to the colors in the other two glasses.

Vinegar turns cabbage juice red. Baking soda turns it green.

Adding soap gives you the same color as the baking soda does. Both soap and baking soda contain a chemical known as a **base**. A base turns cabbage juice green. A base, like the one in soap, also stings your eyes. Vinegar contains a chemical known as an **acid**. An acid turns cabbage juice red.

Experiment to see what else you have at home that might be an acid or a base. You can tell by checking the color after you add each substance to the cabbage juice. Are there other colors, besides green, that can you see when you use soap in an experiment?

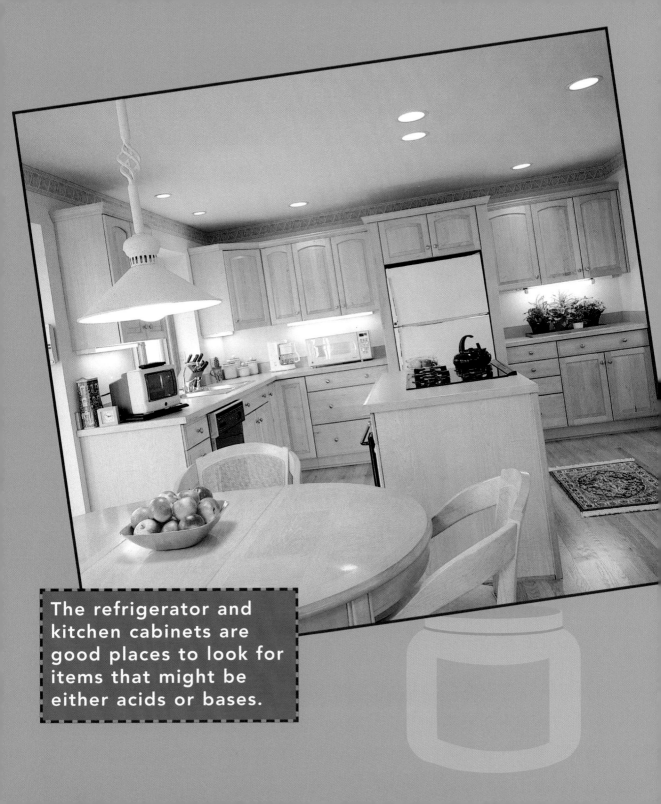

The refrigerator and kitchen cabinets are good places to look for items that might be either acids or bases.

Seeing Colors

You will need:
- large bottle of soap bubble solution
- flashlight
- dark room or closet

Practice blowing soap bubbles so that they do not fall off the wand. Bring the bubble liquid and flashlight into a closet or darken the room completely. Use one hand to hold the flashlight in front of your eyes with the light shining on the ceiling.

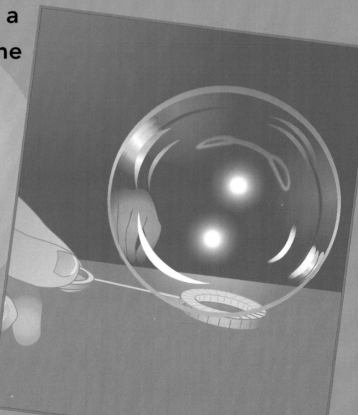

Use your other hand to blow a large bubble that stays on the wand. Slowly move the wand over the flashlight. Look closely at the bubble. How many colors do you see? Do the colors change as you look at them?

A soap bubble is like a ham sandwich. A bubble has two layers of soap, just like the sandwich has two slices of bread. Between the two soap layers, there is a layer of water, just like the layer of ham in the sandwich.

White light, like the light from a flashlight, actually contains all the colors of the rainbow. When white light bounces off the two soap layers in a bubble, it produces the colors you see. Because of the way the light bounces, the colors keep changing as you look at them.

Water droplets in the air break up sunlight into all the colors that you see in a rainbow.

What Can You Learn From Soap Bubbles?

Blowing soap bubbles can be a lot of fun. It can also be a way to carry out some experiments and learn something. See how you can use a soap bubble to find out how much air is in your lungs.

Measuring the Air

You will need:
- straw
- scissors
- table
- large flat tray
- soap bubble solution
- chair
- ruler

Use your fingers to flatten one end of the straw. Cut the middle of the flattened end into two flaps about 0.5 inches (1 centimeter) long. Flatten the two flaps. Then cut up the middle of the two flaps about 0.5 inches (1 centimeter). Bend the four flaps so they stick straight out.

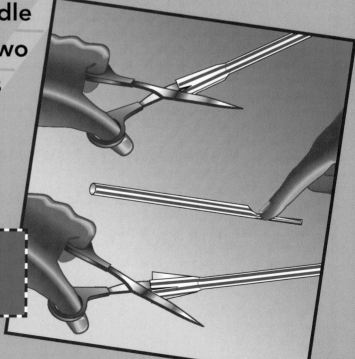

The four flaps should be bent so that they stick straight out.

Place the tray on the table. Fill it with the soap bubble solution. Use your finger to wet all the edges of the tray. Sit down and take a few deep breaths. Poke the end of the straw with the flaps into the liquid. Take a deep breath and slowly blow into the straw. Keep blowing for as long as you can. Quickly twist the straw and pull it out of the bubble.

Measure the distance between the two edges of the bubble. Test your family members and friends to see how much air they have in their lungs. The larger the bubble, the more air it contains. So a soap bubble can tell you who has the most air in his or her lungs. You can also use soap bubbles to find out something about the air in the room.

34

Following the Breeze

You will need:
- soap bubble solution
- bubble wand
- small pot
- stove

Dip your wand in the soap bubble solution. Practice blowing until you can make a stream of small bubbles. Notice that these bubbles do not float or rise up in the air. Instead, they fall straight down.

Do not get too close to the pot of hot water on the stove.

Ask an adult to help you boil a pot of water on the stove. After the water has been boiling for a minute, turn off the stove and blow a stream of small bubbles over the pot. Watch what happens to these bubbles. Do all of them fall straight down?

The steam coming from the hot water warms the air above the pot. Warm air rises. As it rises, it pushes the cooler air downward. The movement of the warm air and cool air is called an **air current**. You cannot see an air current. But soap bubbles can tell you it's there.

Some of the bubbles you blow over the pot are heavier than air. These bubbles fall downward. However, some of the small bubbles you blow should be light enough to be carried up by the air current. As the warm air rises toward the ceiling, it can carry a bubble along with it. However, the bubble will not reach the ceiling.

Near the ceiling, cooler air is being pushed downward by the rising, warmer air. As the cooler air moves downward, it carries the bubble along with it.

Experiment to see if you can find air currents elsewhere in your home. Try blowing bubbles in different rooms, near a sunny window, and just after the front door has been opened and closed. Where is the air moving the fastest?

Fun With Soap

Now that you have learned something about soap, here is a fun experiment to perform. The biggest soap bubble ever made was just over 50 yards (46 meters) long, or half the length of a football field. This bubble made it into the *Guinness Book of World Records*. See how you can make some interesting soap bubbles.

Making Different Shapes

You will need:
- marker
- plastic lid
- scissors
- string
- stapler
- pie pan
- soap bubble solution
- thin wire

Draw a spiral on the lid. Cut along the spiral and then gently pull each end of it. Hold one end of the spiral in the air. Cut a piece of string that is about 6 inches (15 cm) longer than the length of the hanging spiral. Drop the string inside the spiral.

Staple one end of the string to the bottom of the spiral. Staple the string to the spiral at

the top. You should
have about 6 inches (15 cm) of string
that extends beyond the top of the spiral.

Fill the pie pan with the soap bubble solution. Hold the string and dip the spiral into the liquid. Slowly pull the spiral up by the string. You should form a bubble in the shape of a spiral. Experiment to see how many different bubble shapes you can make. Use thin wire to make squares, rectangles, and pyramids. Make sure to cover your wire shapes completely with the bubble liquid.

You can make your own bubble solution by mixing 4 ounces (118 ml) of dishwashing detergent and 3 tablespoons (44 ml) of glycerin in 1 quart (1 liter) of water. You can buy glycerin in a pharmacy.

To Find Out More

If you would like to learn more about soap, check out these additional resources.

 **Books**

Barber, Jacquelin and Carolyn Willard. **Bubble Festival.** Lawrence Hall of Science, 1999.

Cassidy, John. **The Unbelievable Bubble Book.** Klutz, 1995.

Ripley, Catherine. **Why Is Soap So Slippery?** Firefly Books, 1995.

Taylor, Barbara. **I Wonder Why Soap Makes Bubbles.** Larousse Kingfisher Chambers, 1994.

Soap Making For Kids. Scholastic Trade, 1998.

Organizations and Online Sites

Bubbles and Balloons
http://nuevaschool.org/ ~debbie/library/cur/sci/ bubbles&balloons.html

This site has links to a number of activities and a list of books about soap.

Salt Lake City Library System
http://www.slco.lib.ut.us/ kidsci.htm

Click on "Science Experiments/Science Fair." Then go to the Baffling Soap Bubbles activity.

Baffling Bubbles
http://www.kcmuseum.com/ xp-sci.html

Learn how to make "3-D geo-bubbles" using pipe cleaners and bubble solution.

Bubbles and Balloons
http://www.ldsworld.com/ ldsworld/kidsworld/ teachme/science/julylab/ julylab.htm

See what bubbles and balloons have in common. Learn how to make "The Best Bubble Blowers."

Important Words

acid chemical that tastes sour and turns cabbage juice red

air current movement of air

base chemical that feels slippery and turns cabbage juice green

distilled water water that contains no salts, minerals, or anything else besides water molecules

hard water water that contains a large amount of salt

molecule very tiny particle that makes up things such as water

surface tension the sticking together of water molecules to form a thin "skin" on the surface

Index

Meet the Author

Salvatore Tocci is a science writer who lives in East Hampton, New York, with his wife, Patti. He was a high school biology and chemistry teacher for almost thirty years. As a teacher, he always encouraged his students to perform experiments to learn about science. The well water in the Toccis' new house was so hard that they had to install a special device to make it softer. Now they can get cleaner when they wash with soap.

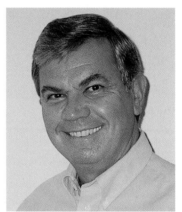